Scholars of the
STORM(s)

Elizabeth Rafferty PhD

Cover image © Shutterstock.com

www.innovativeinkpublishing.com
Send all inquiries to:
4050 Westmark Drive
Dubuque, IA 52004-1840

Copyright © Elizabeth Rafferty

ISBN: 979-8-3851-0317-1
Ebook ISBN: 979-8-3851-0318-8

All rights reserved. No part of this publication may be reproduced, stored in a retrieval system, or transmitted, in any form or by any means, electronic, mechanical, photocopying, recording, or otherwise, without the prior written permission of the copyright owner.

Published in the United States of America

Great thanks to Dr. Robert Connor for his support in
bringing these stories to be heard.

And a note of gratitude to *each* of my international students
that I have taught at Tulane. Their success within their own
storms inspires me beyond measure every day.

Contents

Introduction

Late August 2021 saw the grand chaos of joy and trepidation that comes with students arriving at Tulane University in New Orleans Louisiana (USA). Move-in complete, classes began August 23rd, 2021. On August 29th, approximately two weeks after the arrival of Tulane's student population, Hurricane Ida, a Category 4 hurricane, hit the city.

As a Tulane professor, I teach Composition courses to Tulane's international student population. My courses range from a pre-freshmen experience and freshmen English, to a course in Tulane's Law Department. This offering is a collection of essays written by my freshmen international students in the required English course, ENGL 1011. One section of the course met synchronously and the other asynchronously during the Fall semester 2021.

Through their own words, this offering highlights the incredible tenacity and resilience that my freshmen international students demonstrated while withstanding extreme circumstances presented by Hurricane Ida. Academically, I recognize that their experiences represent the composite of a significant data point; undergraduate international students (non-native speakers) experiencing a natural disaster, (a Category 4 hurricane) two weeks after arriving to study in the United States, during the ongoing global Covid pandemic while navigating the typical aculturation process unique to international students. These factors create the "s" on "Storm" in the book's title. Despite being an extraordinarily unique representation of data valuable for future research and linguistic pedagogical study, my student's sheer resilience became the voice that is the true impetus for this book.

THE CHALLENGES (STORMS)

International students (non-native speakers- L2's) inherently present perspectives in an academic circumstance that first language (L1) students do not encounter. These students arrive from geographical, cultural (both personal and societal), and linguistic circumstances that differ dramatically from what they encounter at an American university. These challenges alone require variant instructional methodology and acculturation protocols that Tulane executes in a historically successful multi-departmental effort.

The essays were written by international students in Tulane University's required freshmen English course. It was the first essay required in the course (ENGL 1011) which presents the typical challenges faced by a non-native speakers first piece of academic writing. The academic challenges include factors such as fluency level and style configuration of previous English instruction with significant consideration given to linguistic and cultural protocols that drive their first language.

Typical acculturation challenges are vast for all students embarking on an academic career at the university level. International students face these same challenges with the addition of a dramatically different cultural and experenital perspective. The social and emotional challenges ranging from peer/roommate interaction to deciphering the food presented at the cafeteria, are magnified when one comes from a different culture. International students leave all that is familiar, family, friends, and environment/culture to become emersed in a significantly variant culture and set of values. Add to these "storms" a Category 4 hurricane and we have their experiences during the Fall of 2021.

In addition to the typical linguistic and cultural issues (storms) international students encounter, we were entering year two of a global pandemic with many of our students having spent the previous year learning remotely. This alone required a significant cognitive learning shift.

The final challenge then presented itself when several days into our Fall Semester, Hurricane Ida, a Category 4 hurricane, devastated the city of New Orleans forcing Tulane to evacuate students from campus, relocating most of us, me included, to Texas for several weeks. This relocation suspended classes for two weeks as the New Orleans power grid was compromised also compromising structures throughout the city, including buildings on Tulane's campus. These weeks away from campus were essential to assure the safety of all associated with the university. Tulane disaster protocols were executed while staff ascertained the safety of all campus buildings for re-habitation before bringing students back to campus. Classes were suspended for two weeks immediately following the hurricane then resumed via Zoom for two weeks until all returned to campus. Most American students were able to go home for that month however due to expense and Covid protocols, however it was not possible/practical for most international students to return home for the short time before classes in person were to begin.

Fall semester 2021 presented a scenario that none of us hoped would ever come to fruition. The synergy of events that occurred for these students; studying/living in a new country/culture, during a pandemic, experiencing firsthand a Category 4 hurricane, being displaced for weeks in the hurricane aftermath then being asked to complete a semester of rigorous academic study is a once in a lifetime event that is still almost unimaginable, even to those of us who lived through it.

HOW DO WE VIEW THIS INFORMATION

As human beings we gain strength from one another's journeys and their recounting. The journey of my 26 students (16 of which agreed to have their essays published here) took an extraordinary turn from the usual expected acculturation process (a typically daunting task, especially during a pandemic) that was anticipated when they left their homes bound for university life at Tulane. An ill-tempered hurricane named Ida, changed many lives in New Orleans, and this is the firsthand account of that process lived by my international students.

Two critical points form an essential undergirding for understanding the essays presented here, it's timing within the semester and any editing of original student text. It must be noted that these essays were written after only four weeks of instruction within the semester (two of which occurred on Zoom for all students), with the hurricane experience occurring amid those 4 weeks. As the course instructor, I met (as is my usual practice) with each student individually once a rough draft was originally created and offered editing assistance prior to submission. They were then edited by the student, submitted, and graded. It was not my original intent to collect these essays for any purpose other than the standard course assignment. However, after reading the final product I was deeply moved. I saw two very clear facts. One, that the essay quality, candor, and content needed to be given a voice, and secondly that there was a convergence of a unique set of data points that created the exigence for these stories.

Additionally, it must be noted that students were not asked for a commitment for involvement until several months after the Fall semester ended and course grades had been recorded. And most importantly I must reiterate that *none* of the student's writings were edited by myself or the original authors after submission. I felt it imperative that if the students' voices were to be heard, they must be entirely authentic and represent their real-time writing.

The writings are submitted here for analysis neither qualitatively nor quantitatively, as there is only one possible analytical conclusion. These students lived through a set of circumstances that challenges the imagination, especially to those of us who support international students academically. Hence these narratives offer unique perspectives that challenge, and should drive, how we address our international students both as learners and as individuals.

The book is organized linearly taking the reader through the events associated with Hurricane Ida. I will begin the story, as it is my retelling of the few days before the hurricane with my students that adds the context of someone who has not experienced a hurricane above a Category 3 (Category 3 hurricanes seldom require evacuation and do not usually reek the widespread damage that a higher designation usually brings). Essentially placing my students and me on a steep hurricane learning curve with Ida. My inexperience with hurricanes also adds an ironically humorous beginning to the narrative. After my initial offering of context, the voices of my scholars take over, offering the true value of this text.

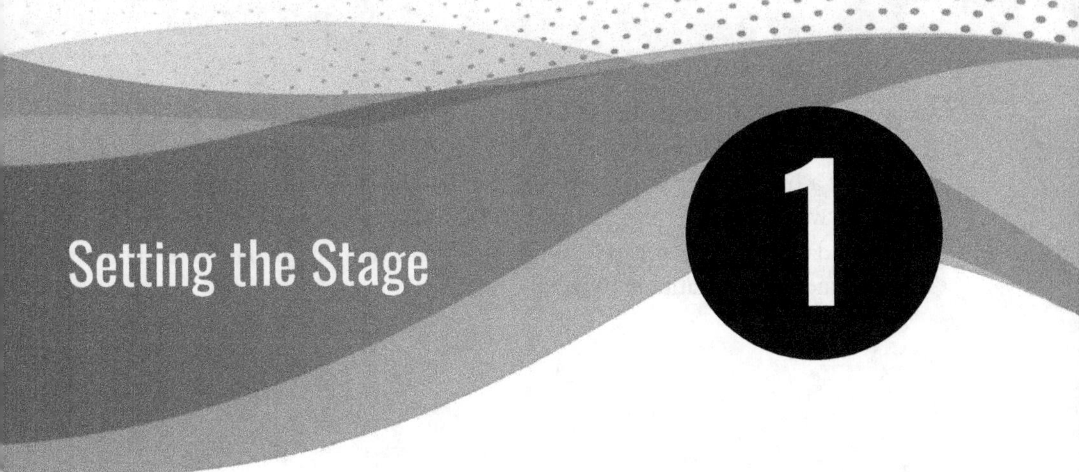

It's the punch you don't see coming that hurts the most. That's how it felt with Ida the Category 4 hurricane that ripped through New Orleans. Hurricanes, or subtropical cyclones, are low pressure systems that form over sub-tropical waters. Category 4 hurricanes according to NOAA (National Oceanographic and Atmospheric Administration) predict that catastrophic damage will occur with winds ranging from 130-156 miles per hour (National Hurricane Center). According to NOAA, Hurricane Ida produced peak winds of 150 mph (Bevin, 2022).

The official report from "National Hurricane Center Tropical Cyclone Report" (Bevin, 2022) issued by the National Oceanic and Atmospheric Administration (NOAA) states that "The genesis of Ida was somewhat poorly forecast." "It was underestimated how quickly the low would subsequently undergo tropical cyclogenesis." Essentially, the ferocity of the storm was not identified quickly enough to execute the pre-hurricane evacuation path necessary in the state of Louisiana, the city of New Orleans and subsequently Tulane University.

We have all watched media coverage of worldwide tragedies. Floods so dramatic that whole houses slip into rushing water, blizzards that send vehicles careening into one another on an interstate and hurricane force winds tearing off rooves like peeling the lid off a soup can. However, unless you have lived through an event, good or bad, it is difficult to conceptualize the impact and its scope. To aid your perspective, picture yourself sitting in the front row of a close friend's wedding. You've seen weddings in movies but the goose bumps that rush over you when you hear "Here Comes the Bride" in person make every video of a wedding pale in comparison. Until moving to New Orleans I had only seen the "pale" media version of a hurricane, and so was the case for the international students in my freshmen writing course in the Fall of 2021. All of our perspectives were challenged, and the concept of "capital" or "value" in life literally changed overnight for Tulane's student population and the city of New Orleans.

Before Hurricane Ida Hit

2

Having lived in New Orleans five years at the time of Ida's appearance, I had experienced several lesser hurricanes but nothing with the intensity of a Category 4 hurricane. Seeing our streets flood numerous times, once witnessing a sofa meant for garbage pick-up float down the street, one becomes used to extreme weather conditions, especially as most dissipate quickly. I remember heading to campus when first hired during a torrential, though not hurricane level, rainstorm. The streets flood quickly as much of the city of New Orleans is below sea level. That particular day the water from passing cars was literally cresting into small waves like the ocean. I was terrified, wondering why no one had warned me. But sometimes there is no way to truly warn someone, you just have to experience it.

By the time Ida was approaching I had weathered the ocean waves in the street and furniture floating past my apartment building, so I felt fairly "seasoned" weather wise, I was grossly mistaken. Hurricane season is officially defined as the period of June 1st to November 30th, so it was expected to have a few "disturbances", (low level hurricanes), at the beginning of the semester in August. Fall semester started August 23rd with international students arriving in the days/week prior.

Classes began the week of August 23rd and it was a day after my first class that forecasts of a hurricane began. Many times, the days before a weather event are rife with catastrophic media stories. So, we had all heard of an impending hurricane, however, as NOAA reports, the genesis was "somewhat poorly forecast" (Bevin 2022). Most of us saw it as a disruptive event, never to be taken lightly due to the potential property damage that always follows a major weather event, but nothing catastrophic. I had two sections of ENGL 1011, freshmen English for international students that Fall, one on Zoom for those students who could not get to the United States yet due to Covid and one in-person class. There were a few students in the Zoom class (scheduling conflicts allowed them to register for Zoom) who were physically on campus at Tulane and we, in our Wednesday evening Zoom, briefly discussed the initial weather reports. However, there was little "concern" even for those students who were residing on campus by Wednesday evening August 25th.

The next day (August 26th) I saw my 2pm Tuesday/Thursday class and I knew that the students had heard numerous escalating weather reports over night on social media and no doubt had received worried contact from their families in their home countries. I also knew that it would be best to address concerns at the beginning of class so that they could concentrate on actual course content.

I started by showing them the hurricane tracking maps that NOAA, had published. We discussed where we were on those maps, and I shared with them my storm stories in an effort to validate any fears they had. But also, to try to put those fears in perspective. (Insert irony here) Many questions later, some involving the infamous Hurricane Katrina, which hit New Orleans on August 29th, 2005 (same date as Ida, more irony) as many of my students had seen footage of the horrific damage from Katrina. I was honest in discussing the unimaginable levels that water rose to in the city but assured them that the levees (levee failure escalated the devastation of Katrina exponentially) had been fortified after Katrina and that would not be a concern with Ida. Before class on the 26th, Ida was still a Category 3 hurricane. I felt that after 10 minutes of discussion their questions had been answered and that we could move into content work and I clearly remember saying, "We will be fine, and I will see you for class next Tuesday." A phrase I repeated again before dismissing class.

I reminded them of this statement after the hurricane event as soon as we resumed classes in person, and we made a joke out of the absurdity of my statement for the remainder of the semester. The fact that they still trusted me after that statement is a testament to the extraordinary character of these incredible students.

The stage is set for my students to take this narrative forward in the eloquence and true candor of their thoughts. "Words can never fully describe our dreadful encounter with Ida which gave me a hard lesson" (Jason Chen). As this first scholar observed, words become almost inadequate when relating their Ida story, yet tenaciously they have crafted an invaluable narrative. Let us allow Jason to begin the journey.

YU-AN "JASON" CHEN

Hurricane Ida Experience

"Overconfidence always sinks the ship." Growing up in Taiwan, typhoons which are the identical things as hurricanes in all nature but the location they form, were certainly a tremendous part of my life. Given the experience in the past, it offers a sense that hurricanes, typhoons, or tropical storms are nothing but another familiar territory. Underestimating hurricane Ida turned out to be an undeniable proof of this old saying in the beginning.

As my mother was visiting New Orleans staying at an Airbnb, evacuating with Tulane was not an option for us. Staying together was the only choice. It was beyond blessed for us to be able to rent a car a day before the hurricane hit. The young couple in front of us was not that fortunate due to their credit card issue. The guy's facial expression from this young couple was full of anxiety, terror, and disappointment that still haunts me today. Looking at the long line behind us at the car rental place, the young couple were not the only people in such anxious mood, the air was full of distress, worrisome and horror. The normal 5 hours drive to Houston, Texas took us more than 12 hours to complete this ordeal with additional stress from time to time. Eventually came the time for us to rest in a hotel in which it took me 40 minutes to find with empty room available. The time symbolized the end of these torments both mentally and physically. Little did we know that this is not over.

Ironically, repeating the mistake by applying previous experience rather than evaluating the circumstances with a holistic approach has led me to reach the conclusion that this was just going to be like a two-day event. The naïve decision of going back to New Orleans to return the rental has become the next thing on our agenda. In Taiwan, the power outage would not last more than 2 hours after or during a typhoon and things are back to normal approximately right after the storm. As a result, my mom and I tried to take the car back to the original rental site and ready to get it fueled up upon returning. When we realized that every gas station within our range is down it was a little bit too late as we were deep in the woods in Baton Rouge area. Without power, without gas, it was lucky enough to find a Motel 6 next to the last gas station we could reach.

Flashing back made me think that this was perhaps just my luck, even as I was beaming with pride, ready to all the glory that is from Tulane and the French Quarter with my mother visiting from Taiwan, Ida threw a wrench into our Itinerary and sent my mother dangerously close to edge of an epic nervous breakdown, as epic as the hurricane she reacted to with so much gnashing of teeth and pulling of hair. The question on everybody's mind had to be, "Would this turn out to be a hurricane that send Katrina to the kiddy table, or would it be a pale imitation?" I tactfully placated my poor mother by distracting her with the task of looking for accommodation online and dissuading her from trying to stockpile a month's supply of provisions and daily necessities, all the while trying to think up a game plan that would allow me to continue my study plan. The highway turned into a hopeless parking lot. Who knows how many hours later, the realization that we were running on fumes edit new vigor to my mother's panic. Again, just my luck the gas station ran dry, and we had to take shelter at Motel 6. We were stuck next to a gas station without gas! While savoring the irony in this very moment the only thing we could do is keeping our fingers crossed that looting and power outage would not rear the ugly heads. The play-by-play Ida coverage and analysis on TV were slowly reduced to wide noise in our grateful roadside Motel room. Coming after were the reassurances to my mother that hurricanes of this magnitude were certainly not an annual occurrence in New Orleans and that New Orleans and Tulane had learnt plenty from Hurricane Katrina.

By no means an isolated event, Ida fits the global pattern of extreme weathers, rising sea levels, and natural disasters of increasing frequency and severity; it's not just New Orleans – all coastal cities the world over are imperiled in varying extends. Her fiery rhetoric and church scold scowl aside, young climate activist Greta Thunberg argued that unless we have a death wish we must, deep-six both the despair that any effort to stand stem the tide of global warming is too little too late and stone code denial that all is well and the polar bears are frolicking, not drowning. The bitter reality is that environmental protection initiatives seem to be inextricably tied up with polarized political ideologies, and thus, federal interventions and grassroots baby steps proceed at the tempo of two steps forward and one step back. Such are the times we live in. We do the necessary though unpleasant or we resign to the distinct possibility that Ida will have many ugly stepsisters for years to come. One can be forgiven for saying that Ida has left less damage in its trail compared to the national trauma that hurricane Katrina wreaked but that fact that we lucked out is no place for complacency. In my book, our school responded to the crisis swiftly and competently and a small consolation is that the incoming students could trade Ida survival stories for a day or two before the hurricane become a distant memory.

The verdant Tulane campus leaves little indication that Ida has visited her fury on the shellshocked community after a brief spell of online teaching. However, words can never fully describe our dreadful encounter with Ida which gave me a hard lesson that being presumptuous and over-relying on past experience are precarious. My mom's and other people's terrified faces still weaves a vivid memory clip in my mind along with the slowly disappearing TV sound from the motel 6. Hurricane Ida has made it abundantly clear that she won't be the last to not only New Orleans, but also the cities adjacent.

SCHOLARS OF THE STORM(S)

The Reality of a Category 4 Hurricane

3

"Last month, Hurricane Ida struck the city of New Orleans unexpectedly and disrupted the lives of hundreds of people. Having recently moved to Tulane University, restlessness was no stranger. The start of new things, new lives, is overwhelming enough; and adding a major natural disaster amid this process may feel like the universe's version of mockery" (Maiah Abadi Sacca). I certainly could not have summed up the reality of the impending hurricane more eloquently than this quote from Maiah.

The city of New Orleans did not execute a mandatory evacuation, only the areas outside the levees were deemed mandatory evacuation areas (Tulane University is contained inside the boundaries of the levees). The issue of timing and contraflow drove governmental decisions as the storm was moving exceptionally fast. Ida gained hurricane status on August 27th over the Isle of Youth, Cuba and rapidly intensified until it made landfall at Port Fourchon Louisiana (roughly 100 miles from the city of New Orleans) on August 29th at 11:55am. Winds were measured at 150 miles per hour upon landfall, a fact that is difficult to truly conceptualize. The storm surge was measured at 5-8 feet with other neighboring areas recording up to 14 feet, rainfall totals were estimated at 10 inches. The damage was reported to be "severe to catastrophic" (Bevin, 2022).

These quantitative measures are used for the recording of scientific data, future storm prediction and more practical concerns of insurance claims/repairs, many of which are still being executed, at this writing, almost two years later.

All of this data is essential and drives future responses from government entities, energy providers, first responders and a host of other organizations that support citizens and their city during a natural disaster. But for this writing the words "severe to catastrophic" are the qualitative measure for what my international students lived through on August 29, 2021. Whether the winds were 150 miles per hour or 124 miles per hour made little difference to my students that terrifying day. The howling wind and pummeling rain coupled with the lack of power, read *total* darkness after nightfall, found them reaching deep into themselves for a strength that I have seen resurface in them long since the winds and rain died down. Add to that the knowledge that their families were seeing this disaster unfold and many students were not able to make immediate contact to reassure their families until after the storm passed. It goes without saying that these circumstances are well beyond what most college freshmen are required to address during their first few weeks on campus.

Once Tulane administration saw the rapid intensification of the hurricane, immediate emergency protocols were begun. Predesignated staff, even though having families and personal dwellings that would most certainly be affected by the storm stayed on campus, many overnight, in order to put into place all safety measures that would keep our students from harm.

Early on August 30, 2021, I received the message through official university channels that all remaining students (undergrads, graduate students, on and off campus students alike) were to be evacuated to Houston the following morning. All students were instructed to pack no more than 2 pieces of luggage, their computers, and all valuables. Prior to this, students had the choice to self-evacuate with Tulane assistance. This evacuation on the 31st took the form of 37 coach buses with police escorts taking the students out of New Orleans to the five hotels they would populate in Houston after the storm (Sanchez, 2021). Storm aftermath photos show students lining up with their suitcases and backpacks at 10 am on the 31st divulging tremendous wear on the face of most. The herculean task of taking 37 busses on the five-hour plus trip (five hours is the normal trip time, this trip was exponentially longer due to storm related damage, power outages and Louisianians evacuating) to Houston was lost on most as they were simply trying to make sense of what had just happened to them over the course of the weekend. Few had slept, but many had reached the charging stations set up by Tulane for phones and devices, offering consolation to both family and friends that they were essentially "okay".

I evacuated the city Saturday August 28th with my family. I made what would have been a five-hour trip with many others on the roadway expanding the journey into a 15-hour ordeal. I cringe at using the word ordeal here for although very unpleasant and stressful, I experienced none of the actual hurricane effects firsthand. I, like most reading this account, must experience it through the words of my international students. And it was after reading these accounts of living through Hurricane Ida that I felt morally obligated to honor their sheer strength of character as I saw them live heroically through the weeks and months after the event as well. Their voices deserve to be heard.

We discuss the idea of "capital" often in my classes, highlighting what has value for you and your audience as a writer. However, I never expected a bath towel to be the answer to a question regarding "capital", yet Maiah brought that to life in a most persuasive way.

MAIAH ABADI SACCA

My Experience with Hurricane Ida

How much would you pay for a towel? Under normal circumstances, most people would agree that a piece of cloth is not worth a substantial amount. However, being in a Category Four hurricane is anything but circumstantially normal. Last month, Hurricane Ida struck the city of New Orleans unexpectedly and disrupted the lives of hundreds of people. Having recently moved into Tulane University, restlessness was no stranger. The start of new things, new lives, is overwhelming enough; and adding a major natural disaster amid this process may feel like the universe's version of mockery. Although physical safety was not a main concern while on campus, the mental burden during the hurricane was overbearing. Hurricane Ida turned out to be an extremely challenging experience. Yet, with the misery came a countless number of lessons. As fierce as Ida was, she proved to be undoubtedly necessary for personal clarity.

Time went by inside the lonely dormitory room as get-readies for the hurricane were being carried out. After piling up on the basics—like water and non-perishable food— and all devices having been charged, the mental preparations for roaring sounds of rain and violent gusts of wind came next. However, there was one paramount thing that changed everything altogether: the damaged window. All of a sudden, a never-ending pour of rain flooded the carpeted floor. It was at this moment that the value of towels substantially increased. Ceaselessly asking (no, begging) for help came to no avail, since there was nothing anyone could do until the hurricane passed and it was safe to go outside. There was no other choice but to act fast, so in a mere minute, every towel in sight was gathered and placed strategically under the windowpane.

In a much smaller span of time than initially expected, the towels looked as if they had been dropped in a pool. Because of the rapid accumulation of water, leaving the room, even just to look for more towels, appeared increasingly more unlikely. Watching the people walking down the hallways installed feelings of jealousy within. Surprisingly, there was no other window in the building with such damage. Still, there was a looming possibility of disaster, and an unattended room would have only accelerated its downfall. The effectiveness of the towels also posed a threat—there was only so much water that they could absorb. At times, the water drops came from the towels themselves, and the remedial function that they were supposed to serve was unfulfilled. The search for the white dove then was frantic; nature was unforgiving. With minimal thought, in an almost instinctive way, the determination of draining the towels of the water took over. By twisting the towels every couple of minutes, the danger of further flooding was controlled. The repetitiveness of this action, however, was enough for hand calluses to grow.

Moreover, stress during this time was a partial result of parental anguish. Surely, every parent's inclination is to ensure their children's safety. It is completely understandable why Hurricane Ida grew to be such a frightening experience. The disturbing distance that separated families provoked deep feelings of restlessness in both children and parents. As Hurricane Ida became stronger, these feelings did, as well. In hindsight, gratefulness for parental support is all that can be felt. The constant outreach should have come as no surprise; yet it did, however, come with much irritation. After all, is it not part of the purpose of college for young adults to leave their parents' nest and get a slight taste of independence? More than independence, there is a longing for parental trust in children's abilities to stay safe and be responsible during conflicting times. The sudden responsibility to tranquilize family members thousands of miles apart promptly became unsettling. Though the amount of distress on a personal note was nebulous, confessions of the struggles being faced at that moment would have only made matters more unstable. The stress radiating through the phone during the hurricane was, most definitely, not a beneficial addition to emotional stability on either side. Remembering the hysterical voices of family members is almost eerie to this day. Perhaps the value of a towel can also be reflected in its ability to muffle the sounds made by irritated people who use them as something to scream into.

Given the circumstances, having to abandon the college environment merely two weeks into the first semester was heart-wrenching. However, this hurricane might have been a small blessing in disguise. Ida hit just before two of the most important Jewish holidays in the year. Not only are the Jewish New Year and the Day of Atonement the favorite of many, but as someone who values family immensely, it was relieving to have been able to celebrate these festivities surrounded by loved ones.

SCHOLARS OF THE STORM(s)

Keeping a mental snapshot of the family sitting around the extensive dinner table and saying the prayers together ensured permanent gratitude and consideration of the existence of positivity in everything. Aside from this familial reconnection, the ability to say proper goodbyes to numerous friends was appreciated. A Covid-19 outbreak that stopped real life in Panama prevented farewell parties a week before departing. The imposition of virtual gatherings on the promotion preparing for college took a toll on many. The impediment of physical contact once again was something frustrating to endure. The return to my home country after only two weeks of having left it came with the priority of rekindling with friends. With the return date back to campus pending, plans were made almost daily to ensure that the time spent at home was worthwhile. Despite the disastrous nature of this experience, it allowed for the reconnection to family values, religion, and loved ones. Even though it was not under ideal conditions, the outcomes of Hurricane Ida were accepted, nevertheless. The decision to consider the effects of this natural disaster from a positive point of view proved to be of utmost importance.

In recollection, Hurricane Ida was, indeed, an extremely complicated time for the entire city of New Orleans. The unforeseen problems that the dormitory room window introduced came with ridiculous amounts of stress. The addition of family worries and their constant outreach during these difficult times were added to the personal helplessness with no benefits. Yet, the reconnection with family and loved ones, especially during the two most important holidays in the Jewish calendar, was a blessing in disguise. During moments as challenging as the ones introduced by Hurricane Ida, how much value would you place on a towel?

Phuc wrote about the "found value" (or capital again), in a dry place to sleep and a plug to charge the device that connects one to the outside world. The building he speaks of, the LBC (Lavin-Bernik Center), is Tulane's campus hub for dining, conference room space and our bookstore normally. But during the storm it took on a new meaning in the students' lives, it became their refuge.

PHUC BUI

Few people have lived through a hurricane. Even fewer people have weathered hurricanes both back home and abroad. As a Vietnamese international student, it feels rather uncomfortable to belong to the latter group. Hurricane Ida was nevertheless a special experience, primarily for the destruction it caused, but also as an insight to the attitude of Americans toward a natural disaster.

The news of hurricane Ida was not surprising. New Orleans is infamous for Hurricane Katrina, and Tulane University have always emphasized the importance of disaster preparedness. Vietnam is also no stranger to catastrophic hurricanes, as evidenced by the destruction from last year's Pacific hurricane season. But from a young age, Vietnamese people were taught the virtues of resilience, a gritty determination to accept and overcome any hardships. So, even as Ida intensified to a Category 4 hurricane, there was no reason to panic. As an international student with no nearby relatives to rely on, my only option was to take shelter inside the Lavin-Bernick Center (LBC) per the Tulane's instructions, and brace for the eventual storm.

On the day of the hurricane, there was no mistaking that this hurricane would be immensely dangerous. Even in the early hours of the day, the sky was covered in a hazy, dark gray, with a few raindrops scattered here and there. It was unwise to dawdle, and students quickly left our dorms for the LBC, out of an abundance of caution by Tulane. Soon the raindrops began to fall in droves, casting a mist surrounding the entire complex, while howling winds swung tree branches from one side to the other. Many of these branches broke, even those more than a foot in diameter. The storm relentlessly battered New Orleans for the better part of the day, well late in the evening. Even then, there was no guarantee that the storm had truly passed, as there was barely any light left outside. As such, one feared to imagine the devastation wrought to the city out there.

The experience inside the LBC was not pleasant, either. While there was a sense of safety in numbers, it was nevertheless unnerving to see that so many people had little choice but to weather the storm. Students huddled next to any electric plugs they can find, and every room was occupied by a few students together with their belongings. The luckier among us had chairs or couches to sit and sleep on, but most students had to make do with a carpet, or even the cold and hard flooring tiles as their bed. Neither was the food something to write home about: it was mostly reheated food from the Commons supplemented with some snacks and bread. Understandably, few students were happy with this arrangement. But to someone who has lived through hurricanes, these complaints came across as empty and distasteful. Here we had electricity and a dry space to sleep, things that would not be taken for granted in Vietnam when a typhoon made landfall.

This is not to say that there were no bright spots throughout the hurricane. The LBC served well as a shelter and kept its inhabitants safe from the worst of the hurricane. There was working internet inside the building, which allowed us to keep in touch with the world outside and distract ourselves from the carnage caused by the hurricane. Tulane staff members worked tirelessly to ensure the safety and comfort of Tulane students. Other students also painted a bleak picture for those who attempted to evacuate from the city: families were separated, traffic was long and torturous,

SCHOLARS OF THE STORM(S)

even the airport was filled with a sense of panic and uncertainty. We were also well-aware of our luck: there were news reports of people left homeless as Ida wrecked their homes, the city had lost power, and people have even lost their lives to the merciless hurricane.

Although the storm had passed, the memories of such an event remained vivid. While Hurricane Ida was well expected to arrive, it was still unnerving to observe the damage it caused up close. But the LBC building kept us safe, despite whatever shortcomings it may had, and remained one of the few positive things out of the experience.

The concept of dark and light crept into many of the scholar's writings. Ceil reminds us how we regard electricity's illuminating power as a constant, a "given" in our day. Especially precious is the light it provides and the promise of what this scholar saw as hope!

HONGNING "CIEL" FU

It seems that the dark was endless. All students lacked power during hurricane night. Although the hurricane Ida deprived their pleasant moods, light, air conditioner, and rain gear, the creative students found solutions.

It was true that the egregious hurricane was stressful, it was doomed to be a poignant night for Tulane students. They not only had to bear the torrid weather but also pick up all baggage in the dark for the next day's evacuation. No phones, no WIFI, no hot water, as students catapulted back to the prehistoric era. The dark shrouded all students' dorm, from the bottom to the top, and every corner was penetrated by charcoal blackness. Compared with darkness, students living on the third floor of Weatherhead said they were more likely to be afraid of their prospects: what stuff should they pack? How long would be the evacuation? The room would be endurable until the next morning? Where would they sleep that night? All questions were unsolvable. They were overwhelmed by the grueling quandary. The negative emotion spread from one room to the other room constantly on this floor.

The upbeat students living on the corner room of the floor, nevertheless, decided to change the passive atmosphere. To get out of the problems, they came up with different ideas to light so that they can put their things in the suitcase. Some of them had small decorative candles in their room, so they were lucky to have a weak glimmer in the dire dark. The glimmer, however, was far from illuminating students' possession. It could only console the disquieting souls. Unexpectedly, one student recalled that there was a loudspeaker box that can shine with various colors in the bottom of a bag. With the glimmer from candles, all things were poured out from the bag. The loudspeaker box was found and booted up. It only took two minutes to make it work. When the student attempted, there was a voice raising in the heart: "Dear God, I beg you to make it light, please! I cannot see anything clearly without light. I don't want to leave anything important here." Delightfully, the god realized the wish. With soft and winding music, the box brightened a small piece of space. The music was played next by next, and the light also transformed from red to blue and white. The student was obsessed with the obscure atmosphere. He was like a puppy finding his way home. Although it was a small piece of space, it was also the place that hope rose. The box was held in one hand, belongings were picked by the other hand. In a while, it was too strenuous to hold, so the books were piled up on the bed and adjusted the direction at a perfect angle. In this way, the box could be placed on the column made of books and brightened wider space. The clothes were folded up and put into the suitcase. Finally, the student looked around the room and closed the suitcase.

This student was extremely exhausted after packing the baggage. It was urgent to climb on the bed and have a good sleep. The dark enclosed the bed, tables, and wardrobes. It was the time to immerse into the night. The night encroached on everything, including the student's peaceful life and study. The high temperature even plundered the last comfort.

Despite the agonizing temperatures, Tulane students created strong relationships during the hurricane. At two or three, the heat had perforated the student's every pore, and it was dejected to be aroused from a dream. It was hard to imagine people did not have air conditioners in the past, but the student could really experience the indescribable torture at that time. The bed was so hot, the sweat drenched the whole pillow, the student felt like laying down in the Sahara Desert with the scorching sun. It was requisite to find cooling. Leaning on the wall, respiring quickly, staring through the windows, the student saw some other students brought their mattresses and pillows walking through the lawn. It seemed that they were about to go to LBC, which offered them food. A fact was recollected: There were some generators in LBC producing cool winds. It was necessary to walk out carefully to avoid from getting lost or falling in the dark. When walking down step by step, the student surprisingly heard some laughter. Indeed, there was nothing. Students perforce found solutions in the plight. As students got closer to the LBC, the brighter the space was. For all the dark was dominant, LBC created a bright fence to protect students. Each step was no longer heavy because the student would arrive in the lighthouse soon. As the student opened the door and got into LBC, cold winds twined around the body. The large generators were working, making people cool and calm down. There were some students playing guitars and dancing to have fun, and they were trying to cover the noise from generators. Many students helped others to move baggage and mattress to a comfortable place, and they were talking about their unique experience: Some students' dorm on the first floor was damaged by the water, but a number of students volunteered to put belongings out. The glass in some windows was broken by the wind, but the students were also helped to shelter rains from the outside with clipboards. Students made new friends in LBC: They found an open space, spread blankets on the ground, sat in a circle, and sang songs loudly. The hurricane damaged the dorm and infrastructure, but also strengthened the Tulane community. Students helped each other no matter where they were from, no matter who they are, no matter where they would go, just because they were members of the Tulane community.

It seemed that the night, absence of light, was not so tedious and eerie as students found ways to solve, notwithstanding the problems were countless: Students got wet in the rain. Some students near the gate of LBC must go out to pick their requisite belongings from the dorm or classroom. Everyone thought the hurricane had almost passed through New Orleans, but it started to rain. Only a few people brought umbrellas, so other students had to come up with ideas. Providentially, there were some large bags containing food in LBC. Students near the door poured all food from bags and cut two holes on the surface. Simple were these "raincoats", these students could protect their hair from water to prevent cold, even if their clothes were drenched.

Nobody knew how long the night lasted, but the sun was rising from the horizon slowly. Students experienced a thrilling night, and now they saw the bright light and the hope finally. They were stressed at first, used the loudspeaker box to illuminate the room, limped a grueling way to LBC, constructed strong relationships with others, and wore white bags running in the rain. It was also a unique night. Tulane students did not await their doom, so sanguine were they to find various methods to rescue themselves. The night was dark and long, but the hearts of Tulane students were warm and bright.

Again, a student recounts how disconcerting it was to lose power, where electricity provided that intangible connectivity to the rest of our world. Jacky's statement, "I can finally have a good night's sleep", reminds us of the value of that ability to connect.

WEI BO "JACKY" HUANG

Can you imagine running with no electricity for two days? I have never faced this kind of experience while I lived in China. This is the first time that I lost power for a few days straight. As China is famous for its fast developing, we only face short outages that are repaired as quickly as possible, never taking more than two days. As it is quite a torment for me because I almost can't do anything without electricity. In modern society, electricity shortage not only does negatives on private life, but also affect academic or industry life.

My experiences made me realize electricity, something we used to take for granted, is actually a scarcity. During hurricane Ida, I realize that electricity is a scarcity since I saw a terrible situation. When I woke up, I saw heavy wind and rain outside while tree hit the power lines, the electrical cables having some loud noise and there is some spark has been emitted from the transformer. I saw people crammed in the hallway, some are crying because they have never been in this kind of situations before and fear what may happen next. I shared their emotions since I felt lonely, helpless, and eager to leave this place. But we are glad to have shelter. After the electrical cables being hit, I talked to my roommate about losing power who didn't think it was a serious problem since the school has generators. However, good times don't last for long, the power went out, right now my roommate and I start to anxiety, because we even don't know what we can do if we run out of light. I prepared to pack, because we think that it is impossible for us to stay here until the electricity is back up. Later, the school emailed us about evacuating to Houston, a city that far away from us.

After two days with no power, finally school decided to send us to Houston by bus. The next morning. On the way to Houston, I saw damaged house without power and people without a shelter. I heard from a teacher who said it's hard to survive without electricity and he cannot do his work while there is no Wi-Fi, so he had no choice but to turn on his hotspot to get on to work. Ida really impacted him because he had to push back all his work and find places with electricity to charge his electronics and make sure that he is keep in touch with the staff, students, and family members. I had a similar feeling of desperation about cannot charge my phone, laptop, and iPad, because I feel disconnect from the world because there is no power, and my devices were running out of battery. After arriving in Houston, I saw that the cities have power unlike New Orleans, and the houses are undamaged. I felt glad and grateful because I can finally have a good night sleep after the temperature in our dorm got hotter after losing power. And finally, when I first enter the hotel, I take out all my charger, because finally I can charge my devices, and I will no longer feel disconnect from the world as I use them . I could finally contact my parents to tell them I am good and not to worry about me. This experience taught me that a person who cannot live without electricity.

Aside for being my necessities, electricity is also very important for industrial production. In addition to affecting the daily output of the factory and the company's income, it can even affect the production capacity of upstream and downstream enterprises and can seriously affect the GDP of the entire city and even the country. Especially for large states where industrial electricity consumption has long been high

SCHOLARS OF THE STORM(s)

in the country, power outages have caused huge losses for workers and factories. For example, in Louisiana, as an out-and-out electric energy input state, a certain automobile tire manufacturer received a notice to mark the date of production on the electricity curtailment form, and the date of electricity curtailment and suspension of production. This one-month production the time does not exceed 15 days. It seems that everyone does not want to take a rest on a hurricane day, but such a rest is anxious and uneasy. Both ordinary workers and business personnel in various industries have revealed anxiety about the power outage caused by this hurricane. After all, if the production line is closed and there is no work in the factory, the expenses of the family and the mortgage and car loans will be a headache. As an ordinary resident, my greatest wish is to live better year after year, and to save some money every year after removing the expenses, the family is kind, and this has been satisfied.

However, in the absence of natural disasters, one day of power outages across the state is not without benefits. At least on this day, equipment can be overhauled. Large-scale maintenance cannot be carried out when the power generation, transformation, transmission, and distribution equipment is in operation. If there is a power outage for one day, all power plants, power transmission and transformation companies, and urban distribution network maintenance companies will make full use of this day to carry out equipment maintenance work to ensure that the equipment will continue to operate for as long as possible after the power outage day and improve the efficiency of power companies. You can make more money if you sell more electricity. I saw there a lot of electric cables and transmission tower has been destroying. This means that the electro companies need large amount of time to repair the damage. In a meanwhile, New Orleans did not have electricity. They make good use of this gap, and then go on the court for a while and then make more moves. But starting up of each generating set requires a certain amount of preparation time. The transmission and transformation network of the overall power system gradually resumes operation, and even the rebalance of all power load and generation load requires a series of operations under power dispatch, and the large power grid is completely restored to normal operation. It may take a few days, which means that some people's lives more than just a day's power outage.

Electricity is the energy source of modern society. It is impossible to imagine what a sudden power outage all over the country would be like for a day. In addition to affecting the work, study, and life of ordinary people, it also has a serious impact on the city's commercial and industrial developments. Therefore, we can conclude that the impact of the power outage is not only on individuals, but also on the entire society. However, in the absence of natural disasters, power outages can help power engineering maintenance work and lay the foundation for the stable work of the power system in the future.

Exceptionally touching is this recognition of the "gift" Ida provided. Such true wisdom Sylvia!

ZHEWEI "SYLVIA" SONG

Suffered from a glimpse of Hurricane Ida

It was a painful encounter for New Orleans. The destruction caused by Hurricane Ida was both traumatic and positive to Tulanians. It grounded university activities but at the same time reinforced the entire community bond, which allowed the fifteen girls from America, China, and Indian who lived on the second floor of Sharp Hall to become trustful to each other.

Students who never experienced a category-four hurricane dread its arrival. Throughout five hours of dark, hopes of a beam of morning sunlight became stronger. After backup generators ran out, all fifteen girls stopped stare at their phones and pay attention to what other people talked about. Each person expressed misery and worries on their pale face as they looked around. Sharp Residential Hall is typically a lively place where girls and boys play card games, study together, or watch videos in the common room. It was changed during Ida. Kindly, people were asking: "how are you today? Did you call your parents? Are they going to pick you up? Please be safe my friends". Boys were trying so hard to bring some vitality, they told jokes. "I thought I can sometimes go sailing in New Orleans since we are so close to the Gulf, but now I feel that I'm going down like the Titanic", this joke was made that night with more laughs and smiley faces. However, it is the instinct to be more sensitive and fragile especially trapped by the darkness of Ida, which acted violently on another side of the door. Despite that, the chatting sound somehow suppressed the screak noise that came from the shaking window. For the sake of Ida, it was the earliest time girls live next door introducing themselves face to face. This precious opportunity was directly generated by Ida, to know each other deeper. Electronic devices, now, block the natural way of communication and occupy most of people's lives. Ida broke this unbalanced lifestyle and indicated its positiveness.

After the power outage, some girls were packing to leave. Tulanians who were unable to travel back home stayed numb and leaned against the wall because Ida was extremely unpredictable to all people. To assure individuals safe from no electricity and damaged windows, sleeping on the corridor and locking doors turned to be the only way to pull through the monster, Ida. People still recall the coldness of the floor. While in the sleeping, girls lied in front kept complaining that both of her arms and back were hurt and turned red as they rubbed the marble all the time. Facing the ferocity of Ida, roommates and residential assistants pass the feeling of protection to each one of the students and were working together to alleviate the tension and anxiety, which froze the air in Sharp. Nevertheless, crowding in a corridor and keeping a distance that less than a meter made people more fearsome. All fifteen girls got each other's back; roommates were sharing their bed sheets, food, and water, or voluntarily holding flashlights for others. Every movement has subconsciously happened. Trapped in this tiny space with full blackness, Tulanians could still care about each other just like a family. If Ida did not take place, people would ever never feel the warmth from the people you haven't have a chance to communicate with. Ida was a channel that mirrored the affirmative attitudes and behaviors of Tulanians. The teamwork and corporations completely showed unity, connection, and virtue. Superficially, this was a negative experience, but it strengthened the friendship and family-ship, which improved single's independence and relationship.

The devastation of Ida should never be underestimated. On and after Ida, at the beginning of the school year, Tulane had to delay the school agenda and shift classes in order to repair the entire campus. However, everything was not set up yet and in fact, it was the right time to know college life and expand the social network. After evacuation, students left classes for fourteen days. In this case, it made people lazier and not focus on study anymore, even worse, students already forgot what they were learned in the past week. Some friends traveled to Houston, visited Chinatown, or hang out with family members, all these distracted them from schoolwork especially for freshmen who started college only a week ago. Meanwhile, for the school board, to replace the whole university community, they needed to move the dates for breaks, exams, classes, sports seasons, and everything momentary. Therefore, for the students who are taking chemistry lab courses this semester, Ida was a sudden interruption that built more concerns and questions for instructors whose responsibility is to re-arrange the class context and assignments, as well as undergraduates.

Under the powerful dominance of Ida, sleeping outside and electricity shutdown are the two benefits, which promote the link between roommates and residential faculties. Adapting to flexible university life, as the result of the destruction of Ida, such as dealing with the altered class schedule, finally leads all these fifteen strong young women to cultivate themselves to be more mature and self-supporting.

"Everything was normal...until..." I can only imagine that the idea of a "normal" day on campus filled with classes, assignments and mundane activities seemed like perfection to the students as they started to realize the scope of what was happening to them. Yiwen brings that idea into focus for us.

YIWEN WANG

How dramatic a role can water play in a dorm room during a Hurricane? Hurricane Ida was severe and destructive. It hit New Orleans violently and affected the dorm rooms. It made the floor of the whole dorm room Monroe 422 in Tulane University saturated. Also, the water during hurricane Ida was still a decoration for people's lives and made students bond together dealing with the laundry.

Monroe room 422's floor was severely saturated by rainfall during Hurricane Ida. August 30th, 2021 was deemed to be an unforgettable day for students who live in Monroe 422. Students living in Monroe never expected how harmful a hurricane can be especially for international students living in the northern part of China, which has never had any hurricane in history. On August 30th, 2021, the sun was shining like any typical morning in New Orleans. As the first ray of sunshine reached the window in the dorm room 422, the student living in Monroe 422 was waiting in the dorm room and drinking the water which was stored a few days before seems normal as usual. The student who lived in dorm room 422 never thought water, a necessity in everyday life, could play a dramatic role in a single dorm room during hurricane Ida.

Everything was normal as usual until the afternoon came. A large mass of clouds started to gather and block out the sun. Winds howled, shaking the window. The sky got cloudy and dusky. Hurricane Ida was about to hit New Orleans. First, the feeling of calmness remained although the hurricane had heavy rainfall and strong winds. Monroe hall residents thought it would not stay for long and affect much of the surroundings. To avoid hurricane Ida, staying in the dorm room with friends was one of the best choices. The student living in dorm room 422 just went out of the room and chatted with friends about the excitement of starting life in college, the residential housing experience living in Monroe, and plans after hurricane Ida.

After walking back to the dorm, the resident in dorm room 422 realized things became strange and the feeling of worrying raised as the smell of a horrible scent spreading throughout the dorm room. She didn't take it seriously and disregarded it as a hint that something went wrong within the dorm room. She laid on the bed and watched the winds blow more fiercely throughout the neighborhood behind Monroe. Gradually, she realized hurricane Ida was going to be more devastating than what people thought. Rainfall beat heavily against the window and there were broken tree branches hanging off the destroyed roofs outside. As the unpleasant scent got more and more severe, she searched for all indications of where the odor came from. Finally, she found the carpet which had turned from light grey into a darker grey and brown color which indicated the origin of the stench. The floor and carpet in the dorm room were saturated by rainfall. What was on the floor including suitcases, kettles, and a blanket filled with clothing were all wet. Also, there was a small crack in the lower part of the window that caused rainfall to leak through.

Dealing with the saturated carpet, floor, and the crack on the window was not easy. Firstly, the crack that made rainfall continuously penetrated the room should be addressed. Even four bags of paper towels were not enough to prevent the leak since the air fraction was huge and overwhelmingly against the paper towels. And paper towels were easily and quickly saturated with rainfall. As rainwater continued to be accumulated and after paper towels had mostly run out, thick clothes were found out to be the best option to fix the leak. Eventually, the thick clothes blocked the leak and fixed the issue. But all the suitcases, blankets and clothes saturated by the rainfall also need to be fixed. Since the paper towels ran out, the suitcases and blankets needed to be wiped repeatedly and washed to clean the unpleasantly smelling water. When the night came out and all the clouds massed, winds whispered through the leaks of the broken window and gradually the outside was dimmer and grayer. The dorm room 422 was mixed with a stench from the rainfall, as the strange sound of the blowing winds and the dark came from the outside and the blackout. The sense of insecurity, nervousness, and fear flooded her mind at the same time.

Water outside the dorm room 422 played a dramatic role even like decoration. Going out the dorm room with saturated floor and terrible smells caused by rainwater, all the people can see a great waterfall decoration located in the Lavin-Bernick Center (LBC) of Tulane University. When the resident who lived in dorm room 422 evacuated from the room to the Lavin-Bernick Center, the waterfall used for decorations near the Tulane bookstore became more obvious than before. It became satirical that on one side the water was destroying a dorm room and on the other side was entertaining people at the same time. Students chatted with each other to make jokes about the stark contrast between the waterfall and the annoying rainwater that had saturated their door rooms. What an ironic scene!

Water in Houston became sufficient but required people to work together to deal with the laundry issue. International students who could not go home chose to evacuate with Tulane University to Houston. However, they could not do laundry in Houston even though they had sufficient water. Water was helpful. But it took more work to do laundry. International students from Brazil, Vietnam, Spain, and China pulled together to hand wash their laundry in Houston. When everyone sat at the round table, supporting each other, and bonding together in a different country, the fresh water they drank became significantly more meaningful to everyone.

The hurricane was devastating because it caused water to saturate a whole dorm room. Also, the cleaning and problem solving was consuming and tiring during the hurricane. But the laughter of waterfall decoration and the water in Houston also bonded international students together. Both the devastating and heartwarming effects of the water during Hurricane Ida will forever remain memorable.

Once again, (almost unbelievably), value is found in what the hurricane provided. By now, you the reader, can see why it was impossible not to share these wonderful scholars works. Skillfully crafted, George is even able to make us hear that "ping" of all power suddenly disappearing in his writing.

JUNYI "GEORGE" XU

Electricity

"Electricity can transform people's lives, not just economically but also socially." This is a sentence said by Piyush Goyal, the Minister of foreign trade in India. India is a country with a severe shortage of electricity, which means they are still one of the backward countries in the developing world. Electricity is close related to our life. For most citizens in New Orleans, the normal operation of electricity is very important to their lives during the storm period.

Simple things will be complicated if human lose electricity. During the period of Hurricane IDA, it made citizens lived in New Orleans feel terrible because of the lost of power. One of the students in Tulane University called George shared his experiences of hurricane Ida. It was a night and rain was pounding his dorm's window as hurricane Ida hits New Orleans. There was a TV show on his computer with a packet of chips. With a sound like "ping", all around suddenly become quiet. Only the light from his computer screen reflected in his face, it was dazzling at that time. His phone screen suddenly lit up with a message from Outlook reminding him to evacuate New Orleans with the school tomorrow. Immediately following the last message, his phone showed a warning that the battery was less than 10 percent charged. As his room was out of power, LBC is the only place to charge the phone. When he got to the elevator room, he found that they could not use the elevator. What's worse, his dormitory was on the 7th *floor, and it was very difficult to walk up the stairs in the dark. Moreover, his mobile phone was almost out of power. By the time he got to the 4*th *floor, There was no light at all in the dark corridor. Thus, he had to take baby steps and feel their way down. Even so, there was a pool of water on the last staircase on that floor, but it was hard to see it because it was so dark. When the time to transfer his body weight to the front foot, the bottom of the foot and the water suddenly slipped, it is easy to lose his weight and fall forward. Fortunately, it was only the last step, so his foot did not hurt too much. However, it takes him about 30 minutes to walk down from the seventh floor to the base floor.*

Losing power was not without any advantages. It can make us have more chances to communicate with others face to face. When he reached in LBC, students sat around a table and played card games around the table, which was very rare before the blackout, because we usually only communicated online and played online games together. On a round table, 8 or 9 students sit around a table. Since a round table was not very large, there was no room for nine students to sit around it, so people brought chairs from other tables and sat in the back. In the center of the table, there were two boxes of cards stacked on top of each other. Cards were scattered freely on the table. It was the first time for so many people to gather together. Because of the power failure, George's switch didn't work. Instead, the joy of face-to-face communication with people, the joy of constantly meeting new people and chatting with friends replaced the joy switch brought to him , which is the joy people can't experience online. It also made him realize that people should spend more time communicating with his friends face to face rather than just online.

People always keep fighting with dark, they are half as productive in the dark. Electricity makes people life convenient. When George came back from LBC and opened his door of his dorm room. A gust of hot air blew his cheek, the air condition broken down. It was so hot and sweat soaked his shirt. Because there was no light, bathing was extremely difficult. People could feel the hot air flow in their bed, that was very disgusting. In addition, Packing his bags in the dark also became a struggle. George's legs kept knocking things off the floor, kicking against bed frames, tripping over suitcases. His whole body has been wet with sweat, coupled with this hot weather, leading to him more difficult to sleep. By about 3 a.m., some power had been restored and the air conditioners were running again. Under the light, his legs no longer have a place to put, but freely shuttle between objects. The shower room can be used again, and the previous stuffy was not at there any longer. With the help of electricity, People can often do more with less usage of time.

In the absence of electricity, people can really add some face to face communications, which is missing in our society today. But on balance, electricity makes people's life more convenient. It simplifies complicated problems. So it's important for the residents of New Orleans to have power during hurricane season.

I am particularly fond of the word "harbor" used in Chen's essay below. Again, it is that examination of capital and what you value in life that can literally change in a day's time.

CHEN YANG

Lavin-Bernick Center and Hurricane Ida

Hurricane Ida turned Tulane students into Tulanians. The unprecedented natural disaster hit New Orleans and forced students to evacuate 600 miles away to Houston. The role of the LBC changed for the evacuated Tulane students before, and after escaping. The Lavin-Bernick Center for University Life is more than just a building. Before the hurricane, the LBC presented itself as a terrible dining hall. During the hurricane, the LBC harbors the anxious and nervous Tulane students, and this experience projected the LBC with the symbol of unity of Tulane community while in evacuation.

Lavin-Bernick Center was an abysmal dining hall which did not satisfy students' needs. The LBC is located in the center of Tulane Campus. In addition to its functions as a dining hall, the LBC also houses various resources and spaces designed to enrich students' campus life by providing student involvement opportunities, house meeting spaces, and campus programming. The official website of Tulane labeled the LBC with different functions and projected it to be an intermediary between Tulane and Tulane student community. Students can participate in the activities held at the LBC after classes in order to get involved in the Tulane community, thus completing the transformation from a Tulane student to a "Tulanian". However, from the start of the school year to the arrival of hurricane Ida, students spent only one week at Tulane, and most of the activities in the LBC did not start yet. Furthermore, students were busy shuttling between classes during weekdays, so they really could not utilize the resources at the LBC. As a result, most freshman's memory of the LBC was it being a dreadful dining hall. On the Tulane campus, there are two dining halls: the Commons and the LBC. During mealtime, the Commons is more crowded due to the diversity of the food provided which gratifies the various taste preferences of students from different cultural backgrounds. On the contrary, the LBC is notorious for its limited dishes, high expenses, and terrible taste. Take pho and sushi, two types of Asian food offered by the LBC, as example. Even though these two foods originated in Asia, they have adapted their tastes to suit locals. In fact, they are just labeled by Asian food as a selling point, the tastes are still not recognized by international Chinese students, therefore Chinese rarely line up to purchase them. Despite the fact that the LBC is geographically located in the center of Tulane University, most students are willing to detour to Commons. When students mention the LBC, the building seems to always be connected with negative evaluations like "bad for eat" and students' disappointment. However, dislike towards the building had gone since Ida came. The meaning of the LBC became different to Tulane students when they shivered with fear and cold in their dormitories. The LBC is no longer a dining hall, but the only harbor that protects the student from Ida.

The LBC is a reassurance for the confused and anxious Tulane community. Before Ida's approaching, tension and stress permeated Tulane's campus. Especially after the Ida destroyed the electrical system in New Orleans, all the dormitories were plunged into darkness the night before evacuating to Houston. With no lights, no internet, and no sound in the dorms, the atmosphere was as depressing as the students' hearts. When students were in a panic about the dark environment and uncertain future, the LBC was the only building on campus with electricity. Because most of the local students had already been evacuated that day, the students who stayed on campus were mainly international students. When they were notified that they had to evacuate New Orleans, the students who had crossed the entire Pacific Ocean to study in another country felt about to leave home, just as they had parted from their families at the airport a week earlier. But, those panicked international students relived their tension when they walked into the harbor, the LBC. The LBC provided not only light and electricity, but also a feeling of coming home. When Tulane students stepped into the LBC that night, they felt like they were back home, and the other Tulanians inside were family members helping each other through the disaster together. For students whose dormitory was destroyed, the LBC offered places for living overnights. Students who had never met before spent a special night with each other, just like siblings living together. Before the hurricane, the LBC was just a dining hall for the freshmen, now it became a bond bringing the freshmen and the school together. Under the protection of the LBC, students really came together for the first time to share their thoughts on the first hurricane experience and to look forward to excavate to Houston together. In addition to the LBC being a harbor for dysphoric international students, it also represents a tangible symbol of Tulane motto.

While the students spent three weeks in Houston, the LBC gradually turned the role of students' harbor into an emblem of unity. Tulane motto is "Non sibi, sed suis", and Tulane University is trying to encourage students to give to the community and to others. Individuals with a spirit of giving are more likely to experience sublime emotions that transcend ordinary pleasures through service to society and dedication to others. Houston's Tulanians were about to face the loss of community and lack of communication. After a seven-hour drive, most of the students arrived in Houston to begin their post-storm lives. For these freshmen, who had arrived in New Orleans for only a week, Houston was an extremely modern city, with tall buildings towering everywhere. Hence, most students were excited that they not only got two weeks of vacation by chance, but also a trip to a metropolis at the beginning. Students choose to spend the first two days of their vacation in Houston's Chinatown, art galleries, aquariums, and zoos. From the photos of Houston shared by these students on social media, they had completely forgotten the anxiety caused by the hurricane. However, this excitement was soon replaced by loneliness. Houston is a bustling city though, but it lacks interaction among the community. Each student came out of his or her room, took the elevator to the floor alone, sit at a round table for dinner merely watching his or her phone alone everyday in Huston. The sharp contrast between the sense of cohesion of the night in the LBC and being alone in the Huston highlight feeling of isolation strengthens the loneliness. The isolation reminded the Tulanians of that night at the LBC. Some of the evacuated students volunteered their card games and offered them to other students for free; a few students shared their chargers with strangers; other students who had musical instruments mentally comforted their schoolmates with music in the corner of the LBC. Although most of the students gathered in the LBC were strangers, they volunteered to contribute to the community. Those valuable memories let students realize the important role played by the LBC, which far exceeds their original impression of it as a "dreadful dining hall".

The role of the Lavin-Bernick Center is more than a landmark building of Tulane University. The LBC started out as a terrible dining hall that failed to cater to the tastes of different students. In the face of panicked Tulane students, the LBC played the role of a harbor to comfort panic souls. As Tulane students spent lonely nights in Houston, the LBC's role shifts to a symbol of unity. Indeed, the LBC is more than a building.

Displaced

Of the approximately 2,000 students originally evacuated from Tulane campus to Houston Texas, over 500 stayed in Houston as going home was not a realistic option. Most of those who stayed were our international students. As with the ferocity of the actual storm myself, most reading this can only try to imagine the shock setting in once, they knew they were safely ensconced in hotels in Houston. How many wished that they were in the safety of their homes with their family to comfort them is unknown, but one can certainly imagine the number being close to, if not, 100%.

On August 30th at 5 PM Tulane began transmitting clear and reassuring email messages to all students, staff, and faculty. Indication that a "hub" (meaning housing in hotels with Tulane staff present) was awaiting the students in Houston and giving the following context that would guide the days following the evacuation. "We are closing campus and cancelling classes through Sunday, September 12th." "Classes will resume *online only* beginning Monday, September 13th through Wednesday, October 6th to give the city time to repair, reinstate power and other critical services."

So, the students were given a new (temporary) home in Houston, their second new "home" in less than a month. Upon getting settled in Houston the international students witnesses most of their American peers leaving for their actual homes and families. Knowing that these peers were evacuating to the comfort of their family home must have been an additional devastating blow for our international students.

As if the actual hurricane was not terrifying enough, now in a hotel in Houston, the students now had another new environment to "decode". A process that was not without its own brand of stress as Phoebe recounts.

YAXIN "PHOEBE" CHEN

Hurricane Ida unveils the connecting power of names. Specifically, people's names break walls between individuals, environments, and cultures. This realization occurred in my evacuation journey after a Category 4 hurricane smashed New Orleans. It happened only two weeks into my first year at Tulane University.

First and foremost, people's names are beneficial for adjustments to new environments. When the evacuation announcement to Houston was published on August 30, I was blanketed with an overwhelming sense of unease. Since I had not experienced any severe weather conditions, I did not know what to expect. My anxiety amplified whereas I had to adjust to an entirely new city. The university set up a temporary dining hall in the hotel's basement, and it became my first adjustment challenge. To digest the embarrassment of sitting alone, I commenced observing my surroundings. The initial thing that directly caught my attention was the grey name tag on the work apparel of this lady who assisted in food service. "Tina" was engraved on that name tag, illuminating a silvery light. Unexpectedly, a flow of shame struck me. I said "thank you" to Tina without looking at her when she put bacon on my plate. I was so absorbed in my anxiety and thoroughly neglected new surroundings. That ignorance prevented me from adjusting to my current situation. At that moment, I found myself repeating "Tina" unconsciously, and my shoulders dropped the tension from the worries that other people would judge me for eating alone. Noticing people's names redirects attention to encompassing situations and alleviates anxiety.

In addition to diffusing attention, remembering people's names to build connections is another essential proof that names contribute to adaptation to new conditions. The next day, I determined to address Tina by her name even with concerns that calling her by name without permission would be inappropriate. "Good morning, Tina." When those words slipped away from my mouth, I could see surprise immediately emerging in her eyes since she was not expecting me to address her by name. "Good morning, girl. Have a good sleep?" Tina replied in an enlightening tone and smiled with her eyes. The pleasure of being cared about made my eyes squint into lines. I replayed that interaction in my head when I was savoring the scrambled eggs served by Tina. I never expected such sweet encounters could occur by simply remembering and saying someone's name. In hindsight, the exchange of words and small talk vitalized by names give people similar feelings to wearing perfume. They feel good about them-selves, seeing that connections with people provide them with a sense of belonging in unfamiliar places. Consequently, they are empowered with peaceful and gratifying mental states to adapt to new environments.

In the next few weeks, I began the practice of noticing people's name tags whenever I was in public areas. "Tina. Jake. Sharan. MJ. Beth. Amelia." I collected the identity labels of people who served meals, the lady who drove us back to New Orleans, the staff working at the Office of International Students and Scholars, and the intern who served as a brief guide of the Houston Museum of Natural Science. Those names diverted my focus to surrounding positions, encouraged the establishment of human connections, and effectively smoothed the process of adjusting to new environments.

Along with the power to break walls between individuals and environments, people's names are potent forces to help exchange cultures. On the bus back to the hotel from Houston Natural Science Museum, I struck up a conversation with Natalie, the lady sitting next to me. "What's the meaning of your Chinese name?" Natalie's curiosity was sparked when she discovered that I was an international student from China. "My Chinese name 'Yaxin' means to consider everything in life as scents that spread far. It's my parents' expectations for me." Her astounding gaze after hearing my re-sponses inspired follow-up discussions. In the subsequent ten minutes, I ascertained that Natalie was named after her grandmother to pay tribute to the humanitarian work of her grandmother. The specific and distinctive purposes concealed in names reflect extensive cultural variations, including language usages and family values. In China, each syllable represents discrete meanings. Therefore, naming people equals the process of combining meanings to develop ideal pictures of a person. On the con-trary, in the United States, people's names could serve as memorial bonds to family members or relatives. The underlying cultural uniqueness renders names as bridges to educational and cultural dialogues.

Admittedly, those connections with new environments through small talk are super-ficial, and the cultural understanding of names appears limited. Nonetheless, the un-expected outcomes of names inspire people to be attentive to ordinary things or things that we take for granted as we live through life at an expeditious pace. After that evacuation, I initiated the process of actively observing the world, especially those de-tails in my encounters with people. Their names, clothes, or even the frequent words they utilize, become inexhaustible sources of inspiration to recognize patterns in peo-ple, environments, and cultures. With conscious practice on observatory muscles and with curiosity about distinctive cultures, people are capable of in-depth explorations within trivial objects.

In conclusion, the unforeseen evacuation due to the hurricane exposes the power of names. Names channel people's anxiety to their surroundings and effectively serve as links to human relationships, altogether making adjusting to current situations more effective. In addition, people's names contain cultural rituals and could promote cultural exchange. With more observation of seemingly indifferent items, people can maximize the power of ordinary things, including names.

Although taking a literal different path, with two different relocations, uncertainty continued to be part of the journey for this scholar below. Being a Tulane athlete represents a serious commitment, and Rafa's observation that his expectations for this path changed dramatically, something that all Tulane's international scholars had in common those early days after the storm.

HURRICANE IDA

Rafa De Alba Valdes

The storm was so strong it knocked out all the power in New Orleans. The storm was so strong it reversed the flow of the Mississippi River.

Five weeks ago, Hurricane Ida's path was heading straight to New Orleans. I had never experienced a hurricane before. Originally, we were planning on staying in my dorm, sheltering in place.

Fortunately, we decided to evacuate late Saturday night, right before the storm began to make landfall in Louisiana. I am on the men's tennis team and the athletic department evacuated us to Birmingham, Alabama. We arrived in Birmingham, Alabama around three in the morning.

On Friday, two days before the hurricane, we had a zoom meeting with our head coach, and we talked about the hurricane and practice, he told us that we could stay in Tulane during the hurricane and take care of ourselves, he also said that he was going to be there if any one of us needs something and then we will figure it out how to practice.

So, the next day I was just thinking how bad it was going to be, how many days we would be stuck in the dorms, how many days are we would be not playing tennis and going to the gym. I was also scared because I never experienced something like that in my life. Later that day, our head coach called us and says that Tulane is taking care of student-athletes and that there will be shuttles to Birmingham at 9 pm, that made all of us very happy because we knew that we were going to be safe.

We arrived at the Sheraton in Birmingham, but we were worried about practice because we were supposed to have a tournament on September 10th. Usually, we practice 3 hours of tennis every day from Monday to Saturday and we do weights at 6 am three times a week. We didn't know how many days we are going to stay there without playing tennis so one of my teammates spoke with the tennis head coach of Samford University to see if we could practice at their tennis courts and the coach was very nice and said yes. We started to practice there for around one to two hours a day. Another question that we had was if our head coach was fine because we tried to call him and text him and he was not answering so we were worried about him. Our assistant coach was fine because he evacuated to Texas, but our head coach was at his home in New Orleans, but then after 3 days he answered and told us that he was coming to Birmingham. We were relieved to hear that. Both of my head coach's cars got broken into. He went from New Orleans to Birmingham on a motorcycle. He spoke to us about his experience during the hurricane and fortunately, his house was fine.

In Birmingham, I talked with some friends of mine that were at Tulane during the hurricane, and they told me that it was quite horrible. Some of them had to sleep in the hallways of their dorms, some of the rooms had leaked through the roof, some people had to sleep in the commons, and they were scared for their safety and did not enjoy their time doing so.

In Birmingham, Tulane gave us the option to stay four weeks in the Sheraton or to go home. After we spoke with our coaches and teammates, we decided to go to the home of one of our teammates in Cleveland, Ohio. We took that decision because although the hotel was nice, we had to buy our food each day and after one week in Birmingham, everyone was so bored, there is nothing to do in that city so that is why we went to Cleveland. Two of my teammates went to New York, another one went to Detroit. The other five of us went to Cleveland. We stayed in Cleveland for three weeks.

We arrived in Cleveland and stay at my teammate's house, it was a beautiful house with a big front yard, the house has a little cinema room with many couches and beds, that is where we slept. His family was very nice to all of us, his dad's name is Alex, he is a strong, six-foot man, he is a tennis coach and a very nice person, he helped us with the practices, and he allowed us to practice at his tennis courts. His mom's name is Susana, and she is a wonderful person, she is blonde and tall, she was always asking if we need something, she was cooking for us every day and it should be emphasized that we were five men of 19-20 years old in his house, that means *that she had to cook so much because we eat a lot. His sister Emma is very funny, she was nervous because she was about to start her college life at UCLA, we had a good time with her. They have two amazing dogs, their names are Totillo and Dailey and they are very cute. Susana takes them out for a walk every day, I also took them out sometimes.*

So, we started practicing three hours every day in green clay courts and his dad was coaching us, we also found a gym where we can go and lift, we were very happy because although we had been traveling and not training so much, now we were training well, going to the gym and we were not in New Orleans during the storm. Also, we were happy because we didn't have any school or homework, so we were spending a great time in Cleveland.

One weekend we went to Indiana University to see the football game and to see some friends, we had a lot of fun in Indiana. The football match was really good, people in there were cheering so loud, it was the first time I went to see a football game. We went back to Cleveland and my teammate's parents left for Los Angeles because his sister had just started her semester at UCLA so her parents accompanied her and they were with her in her first week in college, so we were alone in his house and we had to cook ourselves, go to the supermarket to buy food, clean the house, take the dogs for a walk and train with each other. Then, school started again, we had our zoom classes and our professors told us about their experiences with the hurricane, some stories were bad, others were not so bad.

After three weeks in Cleveland, we went back to New Orleans, we were very excited to return to campus, to see our friends, our coaches, and our university. Unfortunately, our dorms had water damage, so we had to stay in the Hyatt, they moved all the stuff from our dorms and brought it to the hotel, we are still staying at the Hyatt, we are returning to campus on October 11th.

I realized many things these weeks, at first, I was very angry because we didn't know what to do, we did not know how we were going to train, we did not know where we were going to go, but then I realized that we did not have a bad time we had a much better time than many people who were in the hurricane in New Orleans, at least I was with my friends, we found courts to practice, we had fun, we had Wi-Fi, we met people and we were in several cities, in Birmingham, Cleveland, and Indiana in less than a month. So, in the end, we had a good time compared to other people who were suffering during the storm and we are thankful for that.

I purposely ignored the fact that Hurricane Ida was the fifth strongest hurricane to hit the United States in my original hurricane description. I did so because I admired the matter-of-fact way Luc reported this piece of "interesting" data.

HURRICANE IDA: A CRISIS SHOWS US THE REAL IMPORTANT THINGS IN LIFE

Luc Hoeijmans

Hurricane Ida demonstrated what is important in life. Ida was the fifth strongest hurricane to ever hit the United States. It was so powerful that it changed the flow of the Mississippi river. Hurricane Ida had many effects on the world. Its destructive wind and the heavy rainfall were covered worldwide on every news channel, even in my home country of Switzerland. In New Orleans, we saw trees falling on streets, roofs flying through the air, entire roads flooded, and people losing their homes. Even though we mainly saw the horrible effects of the hurricane, we also saw many heart-warming and encouraging scenes. We saw citizens putting essential items for surviving in front of their homes with signs saying: take what you need and be safe, people helping their neighbors preparing for the storm, and cooking for free on their yards for strangers who desperately needed food. However, how did the crisis show us what's really important in life?

Hurricane Ida demonstrated the importance of having valuable friends. It exhibited how much we actually rely on our community, neighbors, strangers, friends and family. On the news one saw the pictures and videos about the endless traffic congestions citizens got stuck into while evacuating from New Orleans. A trip that normally takes for hours took people twelve to fourteen hours Yet, "normal" residents from New Orleans all knew where to flee to. Almost all New Orleans citizens had a plan for evacuation. However, international students in New Orleans had a more difficult time evacuating from the hurricane. Most of them have never experienced a hurricane. The international students had questions like: How much should one pack? What should one pack? How long will we be away from New Orleans? Where should I even evacuate to??? Athletes got evacuated to Birmingham Alabama and were told to pack for four days. Not four weeks. After a week in Birmingham, Tulane decided to send every Athlete who is not in season back home. Tulane did an excellent job in looking after their students and making sure they are safe. Tulane paid for the stay at Birmingham and reimbursed everyone for the flights back home. However, most international students weren't able to fly back home. For example, Switzerland is on the quarantine list in the U.S, which means if one flies back from Switzerland to New

Orleans, one has to quarantine for 14 days. This causes more travel issues and conflicts with school. Additionally, one didn't know when they would be able to return to Tulane. International students were forced to rely on friends or family in the US, to provide them with a secure place to stay during this crisis. Fortunately, I was able to fly to Cleveland Ohio, where one of my team-mate's lives. They let me stay at their house for nearly a month and his mother even cared for me when I felt really sick. I couldn't be more thankful for having loyal and supportive friends. In situations like these, one realizes the importance of others and the support they provide.

The most natural and essential chemical substance in life which seems to be infinite in western culture, becomes from one day to the other a scarce resource. Hurricane Ida reminded us how vital water is. A person can survive without water for three days. If one can't buy water for more than a week because no stores are open, they realize immediately how important water actually is and how privileged we are that we can go into a store, buy water or even just open the tap and filtered water runs out of it. Hurricane Ida taught us that we never should take this for granted. 191 water systems across the Louisiana were experiencing water outages and left entire small communities with no water. How can you cook without water? How can you even survive with no water? This extreme situation expressed us how indispensable the most natural chemical substance in life is and what happens if there is suddenly a shortage. One day before the hurricane hit, my friends and I went to the grocery store to buy water and superposable food. It was the first time in my life where I walked into the food store and I couldn't find a single bottle of water or even a single pack of cereal. In this exact moment I realized how helpless one can be and how flat on your back you are without the normal working system around you. Luckily, I had really good friend, Brayden, who was able to share his supplies and in this case his water with me.

Another example is the realization of how essential electricity is. Without lights, how can you see in your house when it's dark outside? Or work without power to charge your precious phone and laptop. The fridge doesn't work so you can't store your favorite yoghurts anymore. No internet, so how can you communicate with your beloved ones? The loss of power is one of the most severe aftermath-effects of the hurricane. It brings various problems with it. For example, what happens when the back-up generators of certain institutions like the hospital fail? How will you treat emergency patients or even keep the respirators going for patients suffering severe symptoms of Covid-19? Or, how does the food store keep its food cold and prevent it from expiring? People that have gone through numerous of hurricanes know how to prepare for such situations. They buy portable charges, candles, superposable food, a lot of water and maybe even get the walkie-talkie out of the old junk box. But people like myself, that just moved to New Orleans, have never experienced a hurricane and are not *as prepared as others. We don't know what we will need for such a situation or how to behave and act in such a crisis. Nevertheless, myself and others will learn during the crisis what's really important in life. The Head Coach of the Men's Tennis Team from Tulane, Mark Booras, wasn't reachable for several days and we didn't hear from him for four days. My team and I were terribly worried about him because we didn't know if something had happened to him or to his family. After he evacuated to Lafayette, he was able to call us and let us know that he was safe and that his house wasn't damaged. Especially in today's society where we rely on modern technology, the loss of power showed us how important it became over the past 40 years and how challenging it is to live without it, actually it showed us that it nearly got impossible to live without electricity.*

In every crisis there are a few people that take advantage of the chaotic situation. In the hurricane Ida crisis, Tulane hired an external company to check the student's rooms for water damage. They packed and put student's belongings away if their rooms were affected by the hurricane. Some workers however saw an opportunity to make fast money, they took items that they thought were valuable. I personally was affected by this, my favorite watch, which my mother bought 30 years ago got stolen. It was a gift from her and had great emotional value to me.

Hurricane Ida and its crisis showed us in several ways what's really important in life. A key lesson learned is to not take everything for granted. It showed us how import-ant electricity became over the past decades and what happens if we suddenly lose. It taught people to see our water systems and our standard of living as a privilege. Even though my watch got stolen, the crisis reminded me that we live in a caring community where we help each other out and that I'm grateful for everyone and for everything that I have.

"It was like there were invisible hands pushing me forward." This marvelous image that Christina offers says everything. When we lose all control of our daily events, what does one do? Again, the answer I can confidently present is that these scholars resumed life after the storm with a grace that was nothing short of extraordinary.

HURRICANE IDA

Zixin "Christina" Peng

What benefits can housework bring to people? Most people feel that housework is nothing but an unpleasant duty without any benefit. They just have to do it to avoid living in the garbage. Fortunately, modern life now is full of advanced machines.

The dishwasher is responsible for removing the oil stains on the tableware and doing ultraviolet disinfection for them. The vacuum cleaner is responsible for cleaning the dust and falling hair on the floor, and the washing machine is responsible for cleaning the clothes. The industrial revolution and the rapid development of science and technology after that have brought too much convenience and leisure time to people's life, but after a hurricane, some concepts about housework have been refreshed in my mind. Doing housework can bring peace to people's hearts.

On a very ordinary day, many emails about the same theme suddenly popped out of everyone's outlook. The message transmitted to students that they would evacuate because of a once-in-a-century severe storm, which was enough to destroy the lives of people living in this city. Of course, its impact also included the staff, teachers and students of the Tulane university. At that time, as a person who had gone through COVID-19 and had her first school year spent in the online classes (some people also called it Zoom University), it seemed that the storm did not cause much threat. At most, the vacation was advanced, didn't it? But the next development was unexpected. The storm did not destroy this strong campus, however the school has a stand-by generator, which was not enough to continuously support every equipment keep working. It would take the whole city a month to repair the problem of total power failure. The once-in-a-century hurricane finally showed her power and brought trauma to the city.

Students who followed the school evacuation to Houston, including me, came to this city noticing its completely different tone from New Orleans. Some of us were uneasy in the face of the unknown life, and some were very excited and ready to explore a new city. My mood did not experience great ups and downs, Because this sudden holiday, like the past storm, happened without time for preparation. It was like there were invisible hands pushing me forward. In the first evening after the arrival, me lying on a bed that was much larger than the dormitory's in the hotel, looking at the suitcase spread out on the ground, found out that eventually dirty clothed needed to be cleaned. The hotel didn't provide laundry service, and my clothes were not that delicate that needed dry cleaners outside. It turned out these clothes have to be washed with my own hands. Why did this idea make me feel uncomfortable? When this idea came out, part of me felt absurd, because hand washing is the most traditional way. My mind noticed hurricanes have isolated some of the scientific and technological means that people rely on for survival and daily life.

Wetting my clothes with water and then applying soap on the fabric actually calmed my head. This process was very novel. At the same time, wondering whether people haven't done manual work like washing clothes for a long time like me. Everyone has experienced the touch of soap and clothes, but is it true? Do people really feel the smell of soap and the water rushing through their hands every time they wash their hands? Just like when people have dinner, do they pay more attention to food or the content that they chat with friends? Spent a lot of time in the process of washing, drying and repeating clothes was not like the thing the past me would do. Before the hurricane, the washing machine and dryer in the dormitory were my first choice. It was so clear that the touch of the soaked cloth, the smooth foam and the temperature of the water that one could feel. Finally, focusing in washing gave me the sense of reality about being in a strange city. The imperceptible tension and uneasiness blocked my detection system. On the contrary, the process of washing clothes released my pressure and gave me a sense of calm and harmonious happiness.

At ordinary times, throwing all my clothes into the washing machine and let it do the work was on my daily to do list. Me as usual would use these time to read and do some homework, but my brain also needs a chance to breathe. Housework such as washing clothes actually allows people to temporarily escape the external disturbance. People's brains not only relax when they wash clothes, but also get the opportunity to be"distracted". It is this distraction that makes the brain complete some of the most unexpected creations, just like why many singers say they always have inspiration when they are taking a bath. Focusing on the monotonous daily life can help people calm their complex thoughts and achieve the effect of meditation. Mindfulness is not a ritual that requires a special occasion. It is not independent of life, but a part of life.

Of course, not everyone should love doing housework. Machines are faster and have complete functions. Many people need more rest time than a life full of housework. However, this hurricane makes me understand the meaning of housework. Before that, as a person basically didn't have any chance to do housework by myself. It reminds us that if we face it with a proper attitude, These trivial tasks can also become a treasure ground for the birth of mindfulness and creativity.

After the hurricane, me losing a period of time that with a washing machine, learned that doing housework can calm people's mind and bring inspiration. Although the cumbersome and excessive housework does bring inconvenience to daily life, people may consider to choose a different attitude to face the same thing.

Life after Ida

5

Classes resumed online September 13, 2021. For two weeks while campus was being assessed and repairs begun from hurricane damage we met via Zoom. I cannot describe the incredible relief it was just to see my students faces, even if only online. I was extremely anxious to get back to the classroom with my students as it somehow represented a milestone signifying that the worst was behind us, even for my Zoom students.

I knew that my students would return to campus with some trepidation and curiosity. I stayed in Houston for 5 days, returning 24 hours before power returned to my portion of the city. I had lived in Houston in an almost "vacation-like" mind set. Plenty of restaurants to visit, museums to explore, general sites to be seen. However, there was a looming unreal world waiting for me at home in New Orleans, an idea that was seldom far from my thoughts. As my family and I drove toward New Orleans, this "reality" began to unfold, first in vegetation along the highway appearing to have received damage then moving to large swaths of trees uprooted as if in some science fiction film "devastation event". But the real devastation lay ahead in the heartbreak of some streets still filled with standing water, and houses crumpled as if some enormous boulder had been hurled in their direction. The roof of a well known brewery in New Orleans French Quarter having its roof wrenched off and tossed into a nearby intersection where on a normal day one would find tourists exploring the city stood as one symbol of the ferocity of nature that we often underestimate.

I hold deep affection for the city of New Orleans; I have never felt more welcome nor loved than in this city. And if I ever needed evidence of why, I saw it played out in the days following Ida. Days where I saw what we New Orleanians are truly made of. Countless social media posts appeared from people all over the city, grilling what food they had left, not all power being restored immediately, and everyone emptying their freezers and feeding their neighbors. Posts of bottled water, (city pumps were down, so no drinking water), invited people to come and take what they needed from neighbors' porches at no cost. Grand barbeques in every neighborhood with exquisite menus to use food that would soon spoil without refrigeration lavished on anyone who wanted/needed to come and share a meal. And the most vivid post for me was from a young family expecting a baby in the late fall of 2021. They offered their new crib and all its appointments to anyone who had a baby with no place to sleep, mankind at its most compassionate.

Seeing this stunning sense of community spurred me to create a short movie containing all of these social media posts so that my students would see what they were coming back to. The physical devastation of the city was difficult to witness, I wanted to offset those scenes with the beauty of the people who are the city of New Orleans. I wanted my brave warriors, (hardly an execration of verbiage after what they had been through), to see that they belonged to this unique and admirable culture of New Orleans.

Yichu eloquently addresses the ultimate question, *"How did Hurricane Ida change our life?"*

YICHU HOU

How did Hurricane Ida change our life?

Have you ever experienced a hurricane? The first hurricane I experienced brought me what seemed like endless darkness. Hurricane Ida, which landed on August 29, 2021, completely changed people's lives. Hurricane Ida caused a large power outage in New Orleans, which made our lives dark and inconvenient, but power outages also made us pay more attention to interpersonal relationships.

The power outage brought life back to the inconvenient dark age. When Hurricane Ida hit the New Orleans area, the government was afraid that the hurricane would blow off the wires with high-voltage electricity. Therefore, New Orleans area stopped power supply. The hurricane entrained heavy rain and devastated everything outdoors, the house was extremely sultry. The power outage not only made the room dark and no light, but also cut off the operation of the air conditioner. The power outage brought a lot of inconvenience. As usual, in spare time, people always use computers to connect to the Internet, watch various news on the Internet, play social media on their cellphones, and watch TV shows. However, during the outage, there was no Wi-Fi, no internet, and the lights were gone, and the world seemed to be suspended. People would know the silence in the night is terrifying and terrifying when they spend a long time in the quiet night. The long dark night would make people feel as if there is someone standing behind you, but you don't know it. Moreover, dark would make people overthink, think about the past life, and recall some unpleasant things, which could make you fall into infinite sadness. Especially, a person lives by himself, the strange silence would be infinitely magnified. The power outage caused by hurricane Ida made our lives dark and dangerous.

However, power outages also brought closer relationships with friends or family around people. During outage, people couldn't update Instagram and other social media or applications on the Internet. The outage kept Wi-Fi out of work and cut off the Internet connection. So, people only can chat with are their friends and neighbors. The hurricane caused busy people at work to put down their work, and the pace of life became slower, which gave people the opportunity to have more conversations with their neighbors and family. In modern society, the pace of life is becoming faster and faster, and people are becoming more and more alienated. Whether it is with their friends or family, it seems that they have to wait for weekends or holidays to let everyone have time to sit and communicate some interesting things in their lives. However, the large-scale outage caused by the hurricane brought everyone together and allowed everyone to chat in their houses. For example, for students who just entered the Tulane university. In order to protect students from the damage caused by the hurricane, Tulane University required everyone to leave their bedroom and sat in the corridor to stay away from the glass that might be damaged by the hurricane. In the corridor, everyone can comfort each other without worrying about the danger brought by the hurricane, students can introduce themselves and meet new friends. If someone encountered any difficulty, everyone could help each other. Although the hall was dark, everyone re-ignited their lights with flashlights or lighted stuff, and they were happily playing card and Sudoku games together. The students met some new friends during the outage. The power outage allowed everyone to understand each other better, but it also allowed everyone to have a lot of new "hurricane friends".

One month later, students and residents back to the fully powered campus. Although the pace of life has accelerated and people are still more willing to find each other through network software, the friendships that people built during the hurricane still exist. When people walk on campus now and meet "hurricane friends", they will greet each other, they are no longer strangers, but warm friends who have ex-

perienced a powerful natural disaster. The hurricane changed our friends and also changed our lives.

In general, although the power outage caused by hurricane "Ida" has brought us "hurricane friends" and also made us have closer relationships with neighbors and friends, it has made our lives dangerous and dark. Hurricane "Ida" destroyed our city, caused serious property damage, and made people homeless. Hurricane, as one of the most dangerous natural disasters in the world, humans still have to learn how to protect themselves from hurricanes as much as possible and minimize the damage to cities caused by hurricanes.

Jason's phrase, "intense conflict of the expectations" demonstrates the critical thinking skills we strive to instill in our scholars at Tulane. It was not only the power grid and the physical structures that were compromised, but the very core of expectations for each of Tulane's students. Expectations that were created over months, perhaps years prior to physically embarking on their university journey.

PEILIN "JASON" YE

"Tulane Alerts: Off Campus Student Evacuation", the alarming email headline of hurricane Ida shocked all of the students. The hurricane Ida seriously affected the living experience on campus, which diverged the perspectives. This exigence brought tension to Chinese Tulane freshmen because of the environment, communication, and learning state. The actual campus environment conflicted with the expectations.

Hurricane Ida damaged the Tulane environment of living and studying. The exhaustion from a sixteen-hour long flight could not overpower the desire to seek for a better environment in New Orleans. But the category-four hurricane unpredictably destroyed all of the expectations for college life. Almost instantaneously, the inner conflict and heightened stress were activated after the appearance of this natural disaster. It was extremely harsh to witness that the sunny and refreshing atmosphere of the city now has fallen to become a place with an uninhabitable climate. For that period of disaster and the later recovery of the infrastructures, complaints, distress, and sadness swirled up the minds. Seeing the exhilarating aspects of the supposedly beautiful city being replaced by the howling storm and the pouring rain was depressing. No one wanted to accept and live with it. Trees were torn down and houses were terribly wrecked. The once green, warm yellow, and light orange became gloomy dark and grey. It all happened too quick, making the period of adaptation almost impossible. The hopes for exciting social interactions and some decent meals were destroyed by the hurricane Ida. It was undesirable for the well-organized schedule to disappear, leaving numerous problems to deal with. After the hurricane invaded the city, there was a sudden moment of deep thinking. If the hurricane didn't happen, there would be countless superb restaurants to be discovered. If hurricane Ida didn't land on New Orleans, now students could be immersed in the atmosphere of studying. However, the reality was that these assumptions were disqualified by the unanticipated hurricane Ida. Even though the school sent out countless emails reminding of the significance of the hurricane and provided temporary shelters, it was still overwhelming to admit that those pleasant expectations of the pristine environment were gone. The first thing in New Orleans was not to make friends nor to go to parties but to cope with the destructions brought by an unprecedented level of catastrophe.

Since the environment was ruined by the hurricane, the stagnation of communication raised the degree of tension. The loss of contact with the academic advisors was out of students' control while the disheartening situation already happened. The destruction brought by the hurricane rendered many students so that they were incapable to catch up academic progress. The first two weeks of the semester were supposed to be the time to confirm with the advisors about specific interests and preference of the courses. This would be essential for a comprehensive development in an academic point of view. However, the arrival of hurricane Ida unpredictably deactivated electricity connections in the whole city. The loss of power caused many academic advisors to be absent. Not being able to reach out to them during the most important period at the start of the semester was unquestionably dispiriting. Panic and intense anxiety were raised to a level that created uneasiness. The concern about deciding courses for the first semester was getting more and more intense. As the time went on, the adjustment of courses became increasingly difficult since many of the classes would be filled up quickly. Right after the first two weeks would be the deadline of add-and-drop decision of the courses. Without the professional advice from the academic advisors, course selection was comparable to gambling. In many cases, hesitation and uncertainty caused most of the decisions on choosing the specific courses to be unusually troublesome. Nervousness and conflict were not only because of the loss of contact with the advisors but also due to that some of the advisors were still available while the others were not. This created more tension and even jealousy because course selection became almost unfair. From the help of few advisors, some students received sufficient support on this affair. However, the rest of them lacked satisfactory information or instructions, making the decision on courses to be excessively problematic. The inner conflict on course decision was exacerbated, provoking a strong sense of uncertainty and even inequality.

Despite the advising issues, the level of tension and conflict was elevated since the state of learning gradually changed. Under the negative influence of the hurricane

Ida, the university had to cancel the classes for almost a week. This specific situation triggered a drastic decline in the learning state. Chinese freshmen were all looking forward to the first semester of academic life. Vigor and ambition for academic development were peaking, for which the study plan was modified to be the most advantageous for learning. The preparation for the new semester even included previewing the prerequisite courses. Before hurricane Ida hit New Orleans, they adjust their learning habit to fit the academic requirement within the first two weeks. But under the unfavorable effect of the hurricane, all the plans were disrupted and the desire to learn was harmed to a large extent. Since the class sessions were suspended and the deadlines of the current assignments were extended, the passion for studying was weakened. Although the extension of required assignments brought a sense of relief, the first month would usually be the time for students to adjust learning state, establish the mindset for studying, and plan the academic careers. By losing the feeling of urgency and the supervision from professors, it became an intense mental struggle. Whether to progressively lose the strong desire to achieve academic goals or to keep planning ahead than other students became exceptionally difficult to decide. Freshmen planned to maximize the time for studying, but the original schedule of the semester was damaged. Under this status quo, whether it is possible to catch up with the academic progress and continue that strong sense of studying became an uncertainty. With these internal struggles, the extent of deteriorating self-control and confidence was interrupting. The weakening of the learning state created potential problems for the academic development. The original level of motivation at the start of the semester became impaired, making it harder to achieve the same degree of stimulation when the courses start again. The hurricane negatively affected the study plan, undermining the purpose for efficient academic development during the first semester of college.

The arrival of hurricane Ida fostered intense conflict of the expectations for the new environment and college life. The inner struggling was aggravated since the communication with academic advisors was held in abeyance. It was arduous for Chinese Tulane freshmen to adjust learning state at the beginning of the semester under the harsh hurricane.

"Understanding a city is a slow cumulative process", I marvel at Zhiqing's words as they demonstrate an eloquence of thought reaching well beyond a mere two weeks in the city. New Orleans is a distinct travel destination for many reasons, among them the world class music and food. Anticipating this in addition to the excitement of the university atmosphere then having it literally disappear in a day, just imagine.

ZHIQING YU

Cosmopolitan Hurricane

Leaves swaying, the trees become vertical. This is the first time many Tulane students encountered the hurricane in person, the influence of this natural disaster is fierce: all Tulane students are forced to evacuate. Although the hurricane Ida was disruptive, it gave every student in Tulane University the chance to explore other cities and bond as a real community.

All Tulane students received an email notification the first day Hurricane Ida has passed: Hurricane Ida made destructive damage to power grid in New Orleans city, all students are required to evacuate though they just arrived their campus for a week. In fact, all the residential buildings have been out of power since hurricane Ida made landfall. The next day, all students lined up on the lawn in front of the gymnasium with their packed luggage. While the students were waiting in line, some media rushed to be there for the first-hand information. The photographer was carrying the camera on his shoulders, moving around shooting the surrounding scenes: For million landmarks were reconfigured. This is just the scenes on the campus, most of the buildings are not obviously damaged, but many fallen trees. But for the entire city of New Orleans, many familiar scenes in the past have been destroyed by hurricane. Some classmates in the crowd are still looking around with curious eyes, because some of them have just arrived at this school for a week. Actually, many of them have just learned how to go to LBC, or they have just met the gym in front of them and have made a fitness plan. Seven days, those were the total times they had to meet their university. Many students sighed, moving luggage to the side of the bus mechanically, but stepped onto the bus silently; one bus after another frustrated drove towards coastline. Hurricane Ida forced a halt to the beginning of college life, and Tulane students started their Houston evacuation time from that day.

Understanding a city is a slow cumulative process, however, Hurricane Ida gives this experience as a present to Tulane students: for students who decide to go to Houston with school Tulane offered one month hotel. For other students who go to other cities, Tulane also announce two weeks canceled classes holiday. After a seven-hour drive, everyone arrived in Houston hotel. Although everyone is tired, curiosity and excitement about the new city are still reflected in the face. In the past two weeks, without the troubles of schoolwork and hurricanes, students can enjoy the holiday and explore a new city to the greatest extent. Houston is the fourth largest city in the United States. Downtown is much larger than New Orleans. It also has one of the best Chinatowns in the United States, where students can eat the hometown cuisine they have missed for a long time. In addition to student's own exploration, Tulane also offered school activities: provided bus go to mall, field trips to NASA, and shut-

tles go to airport. When many students left Houston, they already knew many famous local attractions in Houston. Almost everyone went to Nasa to feel the charm of outer space, as well as the nearby Rice University. Some students also chose to go to other places besides Houston, or to visit friends, or to enjoy the vacation. Generally, students were all comforted by the disaster. Many classmates' friends are also in Houston, and this unexpected holiday gave them a chance to reunite. The students live in a hotel. Compared with the scattered dormitories on campus, everyone has more contacts and many new friendships are born. The hurricane gave students a vacation to explore, reunite, and enjoy their unexpected university life.

When the wind blows, it sometimes blows relationship closer. During the hurricane time, school always stands firmly with students. Before Ida arrived, every student's mailbox kept receiving various emails from the school to inform the category of the hurricane, the landing time, and the specific school plan. In addition to mail, the school had prepared a large number of supplies long before the hurricane. Standing on the squad and looking distantly, the LBC is all white, and packs of hurricane food prepared by the school for every student. In addition to guaranteeing food for the students, when the students returned to their residential hall, they also found a lot of drinking water downstairs. Besides school, the New Orleans local area also showed great care for the students. Because of the hurricane, the traffic in New Orleans was very congested on the day the students were evacuated. How to get on the road to Houston has become a big problem. When the students left New Orleans on the bus, the police in New Orleans opened the way in front of the school bus. In addition to the official care of the New Orleans police, the locals also take exceptional care of the students. When the students went to purchase supplies the day before the hurricane, the taxi drivers and restaurant attendants heard their intention to go to the supermarket and gave their experience of dealing with hurricanes in the past: for example, when a hurricane comes, water and power outages are common, buy cans can be more convenient to pack food and it's more comfortable to eat in the hurricane days. After arriving in Houston, everyone in the Tulane community also cares for everyone in this community. There is always a Tulane table in the lobby of the hotel in Houston, and there are always kind teachers behind the table awaiting any questions Tulane students may raise. In the traditional Chinese festival Mid-Autumn Festival, the students organized many activities spontaneously. During the Mid-Autumn Festival, the tradition is to watch the round moon in the sky and eat moon cakes. The students bought moon cakes and desserts at their own expense. Students gathered together to let the joy of the festival dilute the days of fleeing Hurricane in foreign countries. For Tulane students: the school, society, and everyone in the Tulane community, they support each other. In this hurricane, wing didn't blow them further,

Although the impact of Ida is greater than expected, this experience brought the whole Tulane community closer together and the exploration on other cities is also an unforgettable memory.

Conclusion

6

The title of this Chapter is deceptive as the conclusion of this story continues at this writing. Most of my scholars are continuing at Tulane with some graduating within the next year (some taking heavy course loads so as to graduate early, almost unimaginable in light of how they began their university career). The students heard in this narrative now blend in with students who arrived after Ida and often we forget how they started their university journey.

As my students grow academically, they possess an enviable knowledge. The knowledge that they can survive extraordinary hardship while displaying unimaginable strength and flexibility. I often think of these students as the majestic bamboo shoots seen around the world. Beauty in their outer appearance combined with the knowledge that bamboo's tensile strength surpasses that of steel, seems an apt comparison and hopefully a comfort to these extraordinary scholars.

In a gross understatement (some instances in life lacks appropriate discourse), I am immeasurably grateful to my scholars that weathered these storms. I see many of them on campus and am flooded with pride. I see men and women who have been thrown great adversity standing in front of me, wearing the armor of genuine success and a smile that is a beacon of inspiration for the world, I truly see Scholars of the Storm(s)!

Resources

Bevin, J., Hagen, A, Berg, R. (2022, April), National Hurricane Tropical Cyclone Report, Retrieved from https://www.nhc.noaa.gov/data/tcr/AL092021_Ida.pdf

National Hurricane Center, Saffir-Simpson Hurricane Wind Scale, Retrieved from https://www.nhc.noaa.gov/aboutsshws.php

Sanchez, M. (2021). The Tulane Hullabaloo, Retrieved from https://tulanehullabaloo.com/56969/news/inside-tulanes-ida-evacuation/

www.ingramcontent.com/pod-product-compliance
Lightning Source LLC
Chambersburg PA
CBHW060942130726
48001CB00003B/1028